READ WELL Plus
A Great Man

UNIT 21

5   6   7   8   9   RRD   14   13   12   11   10

Read Well is a registered trademark of Sopris West Educational Services.

ISBN 978-1-60218-558-6
ISBN 1-60218-558-1

Printed in the United States of America
Published and Distributed by

Cambium
LEARNING®
Sopris West®

4093 Specialty Place • Longmont, CO 80504 • (303) 651-2829
www.sopriswest.com

167329/1-10

Fluency

NONFICTION · HISTORICAL NARRATIVE

UNIT 21
A Great Man

The 16th President

by Tobi K. Piatek

illustrated by Larry Johnson

Look at the picture on this page. When do you think the story took place?
What makes you think so?

Introduction, Chapter 1

Vocabulary

★ im·pres·sive

Impressive describes something that is so good it gets your attention and respect. If you see something impressive, you will think it is very good.

The performance by the dancers had the crowd cheering and clapping loudly. Use your new word to describe the dancers.

or·di·nar·y

Ordinary means not special. Something that is ordinary is plain and simple.

It was an *ordinary* day. What was the day like?

★ in·spire

Inspire means to make someone feel like he or she can do something good or great.

An artist visited our class. He *inspired* us to draw pictures. What did we want to do?

★ = New

★ in·spir·ing

Someone who is **inspiring** makes others feel like they can do good or great things.

The great basketball player was *inspiring*. He made us want to work hard and become a great. . .

★ slave

A **slave** is a person who is owned by another person and has to work for free.

Many cotton and tobacco farmers used to own *slaves*. The slaves worked in the fields. Were they paid? Why did slaves have to do whatever they were told?

★ slav·er·y

Slavery is owning slaves.

Slavery was common in some states long ago. Is slavery good or bad? Is slavery allowed anymore?

Introduction

Look at a shiny U.S. penny. Whose face do you see on it? Look at a five-dollar bill. Who do you see? Both show the picture of a great man. He died about 150 years ago, but the people of the United States still celebrate his birthday every February.

Look at the faces on the penny and five-dollar bill. Do you know who he is?

Look at the back of the penny. You can see a picture of the building built in his honor. An impressive marble statue of this great man sits inside the building. The gentle face on the statue looks out across the nation's capital as though he is watching over us all. Can you guess who he is?

How can you tell this person is important?

9

His name is Abraham Lincoln. He was the 16th president of the United States. He led the United States through a very bad time. Lincoln is remembered by people all over the world. He is a very important man in history, but you may be surprised by the story of his life.

Abraham Lincoln, 16th President of the United States

Who is the important person on the U.S. penny and five-dollar bill? Who was Abraham Lincoln?

Abraham Lincoln grew up poor. He had to work hard to help his family, so he didn't have much time to go to school. He had to learn how to read on his own. Still, this boy went on to become the president of the United States. How did he do that?

Abraham Lincoln's story has inspired many people. His life shows how one person can work hard and make the world a better place.

Think and Talk

INFERENCE

1. What things in this chapter tell you that Lincoln was a very important person in U.S. history?

INFERENCE

2. What is surprising about this famous man?

ASKING QUESTIONS

3. What questions do you have about Lincoln?

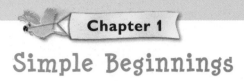

Chapter 1

Simple Beginnings

Abraham Lincoln was born in Kentucky on a cold February day in 1809. Abraham, his parents, and his sister, Sarah, lived in a tiny one-room log cabin with a dirt floor. The furniture was made by hand. The mattresses were filled with cornhusks and had bearskin covers. A fire crackling in the fireplace warmed and lit the cabin. The family cooked their meals in a big pot over that fire.

The Kentucky cabin where Lincoln lived as a young boy

Abraham's father, Thomas Lincoln, could not read or write, but the family listened and laughed at his stories and tall tales. Abraham's mother, Nancy Hanks Lincoln, would also read aloud from the Bible. Abraham loved to listen to his parents' stories.

Why do you think Abraham's family told stories?

One day, when Abraham was seven, his father told the family they were going to move. Thomas Lincoln wanted to go where he could buy good farmland and where people did not own slaves. The family packed all their belongings onto a wagon. They traveled for two long weeks over dirt roads. They crossed the Ohio River to Little Pigeon Creek in Indiana.

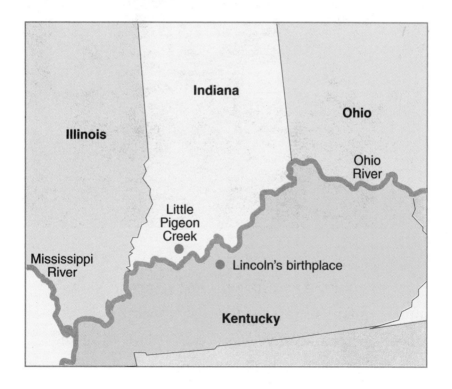

Why did Abraham's family move? Try to imagine what it was like to travel for two weeks in a wagon.

In Indiana, the family built a log cabin in the forest. Abraham was only eight, but he learned to use an axe. Abraham helped cut down trees to clear the land.

The family worried about having enough to eat. Thomas hunted and fished. The family gathered nuts and fruits from the land near their home. Honey from a beehive was a sweet treat. Abe and the rest of the family did their parts so the family could survive.

What did the family do to survive?

Chapters 2, 3

Vocabulary

wid·ow

A **widow** is a woman whose husband has died.

The *widow* worked hard to raise three children. Why did she have to work hard?

★ en·cour·age

Encourage means to help someone feel like he or she can do something. Encourage is another word for "inspire."

Jan's mother *encouraged* her to practice her piano. What do you think her mother said?

pi·o·neer

A **pioneer** is one of the first people to travel to a new place and begin living there. Pioneer is another word for "settler."

Many *pioneers* traveled west in wagon trains to seek their fortunes. What did the pioneers do?

★ im·i·tate

Imitate means to copy someone.

When the trainer at the zoo clapped his hands, the monkey *imitated* the trainer. What did the monkey do?

★ = New

★ gov·ern·ment

Government is the group of people in charge of a city, state, or country. The government makes laws.

The president is part of the . . .

Now You Try It!

Try defining the next word. Then look up the word in the glossary. Your definition might be better!

★ ex·pen·sive

Start with "Something is *expensive* when . . ."
Let's find the word on page 47.

★ = New

Chapter 2

Young Abraham

As a young child, Abraham worked hard. He grew tall and strong. He chopped trees, cleared land, and made logs for a new cabin. Neighbors came and helped the Lincolns build a cabin. They also built fences to keep farm animals in and wild animals out.

Abraham helped plow the fields. He planted seeds, tended the plants, and helped harvest the crops.

As a young child, what did Abraham do that made him strong and responsible?

When Abraham was only nine, his mother became ill and died. It was a very sad time. Abraham's sister, Sarah, cooked and cleaned. Abraham and his father worked in the fields.

The Lincolns were a happy family again when their father remarried a kind-hearted widow, Sarah Bush Johnston. Sarah and her three children all moved into the tiny cabin. A cousin lived there too. Even though it was crowded, Abraham's new stepmother made their home a happy place where Abraham was encouraged to read and learn.

Abraham had no library near his home. Books were expensive, and very few people owned more than one or two. Though he had few books and only a little schooling, Abraham found many ways to learn.

What made life hard for Abe and his sister? What would you do to learn new things if you didn't have books and couldn't go to school?

Abraham talked to the people he met. He met pioneers moving west and peddlers carrying things to sell, like cloth, seeds, and shovels. He met traders, preachers, teachers, and farmers. Abraham talked to them—as many as he could—and learned as much as he could.

Who did Abraham learn from?

Think and Talk

LOCATING INFORMATION

1. What did Abraham do as a child? Look back in your book to help you remember.

INFERENCE

2. Why didn't Abraham go to a library?

EXPLANATION, VIEWING

3. What is Abraham doing in the picture on page 19? How did he learn new things?

CONTRAST

4. How was Abraham's childhood different from yours?

Chapter 3

Abraham Learns

Abraham discovered that he could learn about other places and other people by listening to their stories. But Abraham wanted to know more.

Sometimes in the winter, when the farm work was done, he and Sarah were allowed to go to school. They walked for miles to get there. At school, Abraham learned to read, write, and "reckon" with numbers. Sometimes he found it hard to learn. But once he learned something, he did not forget it.

What did Abraham learn at school? What do you think "reckon" with numbers means?

School learning made Abraham hungry to know more. He wanted to know about important ideas and people. He wanted to read about great adventures and discoveries. The boy who would one day become president loved to read about government and presidents! George Washington, the first president of the United States, was his hero.

Abraham read and learned. Books held the key to the things he wanted to learn. But how could he get books? Abraham would walk for miles to borrow a book. He said, "My best friend is a person who will give me a book I have not read."

Who inspired Lincoln to be a leader? Is there anything so important to you that you would walk miles to borrow it?

Abraham listened to people talk. In church, he listened to the way that the preacher talked to the congregation. He noticed how the preacher used his voice and his hands to get people's attention. After church, his friends laughed as Abraham stood on a stump and imitated the preacher's words and voice.

Abraham listened to other speakers too. Sometimes people made speeches about slavery. Some people said that everyone should be able to own slaves. Others thought slavery was wrong. Abraham read. He listened, and he learned.

Do you think Abraham agreed with everyone he listened to? How do you think Abraham felt about *slavery*? Why?

Chapters 4–6

Vocabulary

★ trans·port

Transport means to take things or people from one place to another.

Trucks *transport* vegetables from the farm to the grocery store. How do the vegetables get from the store to your table? Use your new word.

★ o·pin·ion

An **opinion** is what you think or believe about something.

Tom's *opinion* was that kids should be able to skate on school sidewalks. The principal's opinion was that skating on the sidewalks was too dangerous. What is your opinion? Use your new word.

★ ed·u·cat·ed

An **educated** person has learned a lot. An educated person has usually gone to school.

The man studied hard for many years and became a very *educated* person. What do you think he did to become educated?

★ = New

Now You Try It!

Try defining the next word. Then look up the word in the glossary. Your definition might be better!

ad·ven·ture

Start with "An *adventure* . . ."
Let's find the word on page 47.

slave

Start with "A *slave* . . ."
Let's find the word on page 49.

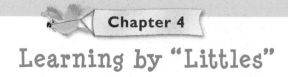

Chapter 4

Learning by "Littles"

Abraham wanted to see more of the world. At 19, he got a job on a flatboat, a large wooden boat used to transport food and goods. Abraham's first trip away from home took him down the Mississippi River to New Orleans.

Abraham had many adventures and saw many new things. In a marketplace, he saw people sold like animals. They were slaves.

Abraham wanted people to be treated with kindness and respect. Seeing human beings treated so badly made him sad and very mad. Stories say that Lincoln knew then that he wanted to help the slaves. But what could a poor farm boy do?

What made Abraham sad and very mad? What did this poor farm boy want to do?

Soon after this trip, Abraham left the farm. He wanted to live in a place where he could learn more and do new things. He moved to the town of New Salem, Illinois.

Lincoln worked in the general store. People were amazed at his great height. His strong hands and strong back made work easy. People liked Abraham because he told funny stories and treated everyone like a friend. Often, people talked to him about the government. Abraham listened and learned.

Abraham noticed that many important people were educated. They knew how to speak well. Abraham wanted to learn how to speak well too. He had an idea. He joined a local club where people practiced making speeches. He soon learned to speak clearly and to express his opinions.

Why did people like Abraham Lincoln? How did Lincoln learn to speak well? What do you think was Lincoln's *opinion* of slavery?

The more Abraham learned, the more he wanted to know. Busy Abraham had little time for school, so he studied by "littles"—a little now, a little then. He learned about history, law, and government. He soon had a lot to talk about and many friends to talk with.

Think and Talk

DESCRIPTION
1. What did Abraham see at the market?

EXPLANATION
2. How did he feel about slavery?

INFERENCE
3. Why do you think Abraham thought slavery was wrong?

EXPLANATION
4. How did Abraham learn to speak well?

INFERENCE
5. What does it mean to learn by "littles"? Why did Abraham have to learn by "littles"?

Chapter 5

Lincoln, the Man

People liked Abraham so much they wanted him to be one of the people who made their state laws. In his first election, Abraham did not get enough votes to win. But almost every voter in his town voted for him! He tried again two years later and won. He became a lawmaker in his state. Abraham Lincoln was on his way to becoming a leader.

When Abraham joined the state government, he was only 25 years old. He stood 6 feet, 4 inches tall and was as skinny as a pole. His pants were too short. His hands were very big. Even he said he was not much to look at. He needed a good suit to look like a gentleman. But he was poor.

Abe borrowed money to buy what he needed. He borrowed a horse to ride and headed off to his new life in the state capital. Everything he owned filled two saddlebags.

Abe studied law books that he borrowed from a friend. It took two years of hard work, but Abe became a lawyer. People said that Abe was an honest man and a good lawyer. He spoke well and was very clever.

How did Abraham get ready for his new job?

One night, Abe went to a party. He met a young, pretty woman named Mary Todd. Mary was different from Abe in many ways. She was wealthy and well dressed, and she was much shorter than Abe. But, like Abe, she was bright and loved to read and learn. Abe and Mary were married in 1842. Together, they had four sons.

What did Abe and Mary have in common?

Chapter 6

Lincoln, the President

In 1846, Abraham Lincoln was elected to help make laws for the whole country. Abe and Mary packed up their little house. The family moved to Washington, D.C., so Abraham could be close to his new work.

What do you think Lincoln did in Washington, D.C.?

When they arrived in the nation's capital, Abe saw slave markets. The sight upset him. Abraham still believed slavery was wrong, and he wanted it to stop. Not everyone agreed.

Americans had to find an answer to an important and difficult question. Should people be allowed to own slaves?

Abraham spoke out loud and often about his opinion. He said, "If slavery is not wrong, nothing is wrong."

People began to notice this smart and kind man. Newspapers everywhere wrote about the things he said. People all over the country knew his face and his words. Abraham Lincoln became famous.

In 1860, people asked Abraham to run for president. He was ready. "The fight must go on," he said.

What was Lincoln's opinion about slavery? What did Lincoln do to become famous? What did Lincoln mean by, "The fight must go on"?

To win votes, Abe spent a lot of time meeting and talking with people. He shook so many hands that his own hands became sore and swollen. He also started to grow his famous beard.

Lincoln won the election. Most people think he won because of his powerful words and ideas. But maybe the beard helped too!

"Mary, we are elected," Abe told his wife one day in 1860. The new president and his family should have been happy. They were going to live in the White House. But the victory was bittersweet. People in the North and the South were upset with each other. A big problem was slavery.

People in the South felt leaders in the North were trying to push them around. Some were afraid that Lincoln might try to end slavery. One by one, states in the South decided not to be part of the United States. They formed their own country. They had their own flag. They even picked their own president.

What was the problem in the United States when Lincoln was president? Why was winning the election bittersweet?

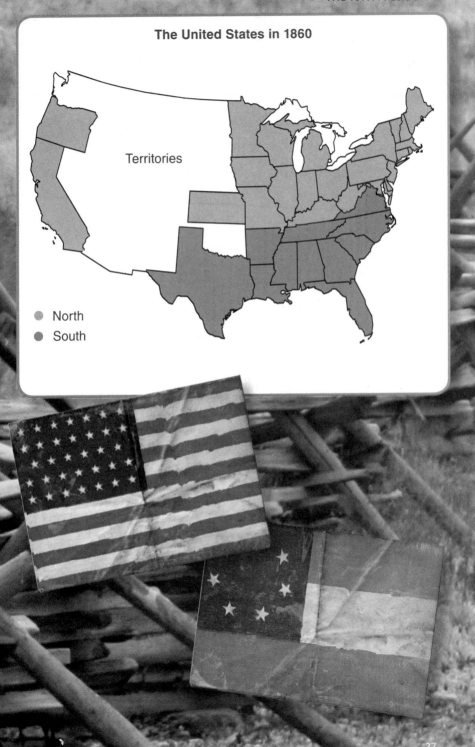

The United States in 1860

Territories

● North
● South

On April 12, 1861, a terrible thing happened. The Civil War began. Americans in the North fought Americans in the South. Friends and family fought each other. Many people died. The war lasted four long years. It made the president very sad, but he kept telling people how important it was to keep the country together.

Think and Talk

INFERENCE, EXPLANATION

1. Lincoln was president during a difficult time. What was the problem?

DRAWING CONCLUSIONS

2. Why do you think people still talk about Lincoln and even celebrate his birthday today?

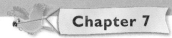

Chapter 7

Vocabulary

★ sur·ren·der

Surrender means to quit or admit that you cannot win.

After years of fighting, the South finally *surrendered*. What does that mean? Why do you think the South surrendered?

cour·age

When you have **courage**, you are brave or able to do difficult things.

It took great *courage* for immigrants to leave their homes and come to America. Why did they have to have great courage?

★ to·wer·ing

Towering means very tall or very great.

The *towering* basketball player bumped his head on the doorway as he entered the room. Why did he bump his head?

★ = New

Chapter 7

Lincoln, Remembered

With the country at war, it was a hard time for Mr. Lincoln and for the United States. Still, the president knew that people had many things to be thankful for. On October 3, 1863, he created a "national day of Thanksgiving." Every year, on the fourth Thursday in November, most Americans celebrate this joyful holiday.

Who started Thanksgiving Day? What do we have to be thankful for?

In 1864, Mr. Lincoln was re-elected president. The North and South were still at war. In January 1865, a new law was passed to end slavery.

On April 9, 1865, the South's biggest army surrendered. The war ended soon after. Abraham Lincoln could smile again, but he knew his work was not done. He wanted the United States to become a strong and healthy nation again.

The theater where Lincoln died

Not long after this, Lincoln went to see a play. People clapped as the president came into the theater. He was a hero.

Why was Lincoln finally able to smile? Why was he a hero?

Not everyone loved Lincoln. John Wilkes Booth was an actor. He hated the way the war had ended. While the play was going on, he snuck into the balcony where Abe was sitting and shot him. The president died the next morning. He was 56 years old.

John Wilkes Booth

On April 15, 1865, the United States lost a great man. His life ended too soon, but people all over the world remember this towering man. People remember that he fought for what he believed was right. People remember that he helped end slavery in the United States. People remember that he kept the country together.

To help everyone remember Abraham Lincoln, the Lincoln Memorial was built in Washington, D.C. It is beautiful and huge, just like Mr. Lincoln's dreams for the United States.

What do people remember Abraham Lincoln for?

A statue of Abe sits in its center. From his place in the nation's capital, he still seems to watch over his country.

The Lincoln Memorial in Washington, D.C.

Think and Talk

PERSONAL RESPONSE

1. Do you think Lincoln is an important man in history? Why?

DRAWING CONCLUSIONS

2. What is impressive and inspiring about Abe Lincoln? Think about how he grew up and what he became.

Fluency

Changing the Face of History
by L.J. Sellers
illustrated by Larry Johnson

Grace Bedell at age 14

When eleven-year-old Grace Bedell saw a 8
picture of skinny Abraham Lincoln, she got an 16
idea. She really wanted him to be president, and 25
she thought she knew how to help. 32

Grace sat down and wrote Lincoln a letter. 40
In the letter, she told him his face was too thin. 51
Then she suggested that he grow a beard. It 60
was a spunky thing for a young girl to tell an 71
important man! Grace told Lincoln that ladies 78
like whiskers. At that time, women couldn't 85
vote. Grace thought that women could talk 92
their husbands into voting for Lincoln—if only 100
he had a beard. 104

Grace promised Lincoln that she would get   7
everyone she knew to vote for him if he grew a   18
beard. She mailed her letter to Lincoln in   26
October 1860.   28

Seven days later, Grace received a letter   35
from Lincoln. She was so thrilled! Lincoln   42
asked Grace if people would think that he was   51
silly for growing a beard.   56

News about Lincoln's letter spread quickly   62
through Grace's town. The community was   68
so proud of Grace! Then on November 7,   76
Abraham Lincoln was elected the 16th president   83
of the United States.   87

On his way to the capital, the new president   96
stopped in Grace's town. Grace waited at the   104
train station with a crowd of people, hoping for   113
a glimpse of Lincoln. She would soon get more   122
than that.   124

What did Grace Bedell suggest to Lincoln in her letter?

When Abraham Lincoln got off the train, he 8
asked for Grace Bedell. Everyone stared at her. 16

Grace hurried to the platform. Then she 23
saw that Lincoln had taken her advice and 31
grown a full beard! Grace got yet another 39
surprise. The new president bent down and 46
kissed her cheek. Grace felt very special. In a 55
small way, she helped change the face of history. 64

Do you think Grace helped get Lincoln elected? How did Lincoln treat
Grace? What would you say to Lincoln if you could meet him today?

Glossary

adventure

An **adventure** is doing something or going somewhere new and exciting.

Sailing for the first time was a great *adventure*.

courage

When you have **courage**, you are brave or able to do difficult things.

President Lincoln showed great *courage* in leading the U.S. through the Civil War.

educated

An **educated** person has learned a lot. An educated person has usually gone to school.

The man studied hard for many years and became a very *educated* person.

encourage

Encourage means to help someone feel like he or she can do something. Encourage is another word for "inspire."

Jan's mother *encouraged* her to practice the piano.

expensive

Something is **expensive** when it costs a lot of money.

I have to save money for a new bicycle, because they are *expensive*.

Glossary

government

Government is the group of people in charge of a city, state, or country. The government makes laws.

The mayor is the head of *government* for the city.

imitate

Imitate means to copy someone.

When the trainer at the zoo clapped his hands, the monkey *imitated* the trainer.

impressive

Impressive describes something that is so good it gets your attention and respect. If you see something impressive, you will think it is very good.

The *impressive* performance by the dancers had the crowd cheering and clapping loudly.

inspire

Inspire means to make someone feel like he or she can do something good or great.

The artist *inspired* our class to draw pictures.

inspiring

Someone who is **inspiring** makes others feel like they can do great things.

The basketball player was inspiring.

opinion

An **opinion** is what you think or believe about something.

Tom's opinion was that the kids should be able to skate on school sidewalks.

ordinary

Ordinary means not special. Something that is ordinary is plain and simple.

Alonso had one ordinary pencil.

pioneer

A **pioneer** is one of the first people to travel to a new place and begin living there. Pioneer is another word for "settler."

Many pioneers traveled west in wagon trains to seek their fortunes.

slave

A **slave** is a person who is owned by another person and has to work for free.

Many cotton and tobacco farmers used to own slaves.

Glossary

slavery

Slavery is owning slaves.

Slavery is no longer allowed in the United States.

surrender

Surrender means to quit or admit that you cannot win.

After years of fighting, the South finally *surrendered*. What does that mean? Why do you think they surrendered?

towering

Towering means very tall or very great.

The *towering* basketball player bumped his head on the doorway as he entered the room.

transport

Transport means to take things or people from one place to another.

Trucks *transport* vegetables from the farm to the market.

widow

A **widow** is a woman whose husband has died.

The *widow* worked hard to raise three children.